Collaborating for Change

EDITED BY PEGGY HOLMAN AND TOM DEVANE

The Strategic Forum

CHRIS SODERQUIST

Berrett-Koehler Communications, Inc.
450 Sansome Street, Suite 1200
San Francisco, CA 94111-3320

ORDERING INFORMATION

Please send orders to Berrett-Koehler Communications, P.O. Box 565, Williston, VT 05495. Or place your order by calling 800-929-2929, faxing 802-864-7626, or visiting www.bkconnection.com.
Special discounts are available on quantity purchases. For details, call 800-929-2929. See the back of this booklet for more information and an order form.

 Printed in the United States of America
on acid-free and recycled paper.

CONTENTS

Voices That Count:
Realizing the Potential of Change

. . . .

Peggy Holman and Tom Devane

As seen through the lens of history, change is inevitable. Just look at any history book. Everything from fashions to attitudes has changed dramatically through the years. Change reflects underlying shifts in values and expectations of the times. Gutenberg's invention of the movable type printing press in the fifteenth century, for example, bolstered the developing humanism of the Renaissance. The new technology complemented the emerging emphasis on individual expression that brought new developments in music, art, and literature. Economic and political shifts paralleled the changing tastes in the arts, creating a prosperous and innovative age—a stark contrast to the preceding Middle Ages.

On the surface, technology enables greater freedom and prosperity. Yet this century has overwhelmed us with new technologies: automobiles, airplanes, radios, televisions, telephones, computers, the Internet. What distinguishes change today is the turbulence created by the breathtaking pace required to assimilate its effects.

In terms of social change, one trend is clear: People are demanding a greater voice in running their own lives. Demonstrated by the American Revolution and affirmed more recently in the fall of the Berlin Wall, the riots in Tiananmen Square, the social unrest in Indonesia, and the redistribution of power in South Africa, this dramatic shift in values and expectations creates enormous potential for positive change today.

So, why does change have such a bad reputation?

One reason is that change introduces uncertainty. While change holds the possibility of good things happening, 80 percent of us see only its negative aspects.[1] And even when people acknowledge their current situation is far from perfect, given the choice between the devil they know or the devil they don't, most opt for the former. The remedy we are learning is to involve people in creating a picture of a better future. Most of us are drawn toward the excitement and possibility of change and move past our fear of the unknown.

Another reason we are wary of change is that it can create winners and losers. Clearly the British were not happy campers at the end of the American Revolution. In corporations, similar battle lines are often drawn between those with something to lose and those with something to gain. The real challenge is to view the change *systemically* and ask what's best for both parties in the post-change environment.

Finally, many people have real data that change is bad for them. These change survivors know that "flavor of the month" change initiatives generally fall disappointingly short. In our organizations and communities, many people have experienced the results of botched attempts at transformational change. Like the cat that jumps on a hot stove only once, it's simple human nature to avoid situations that cause pain. And let's face it, enough change efforts have failed to create plenty of cynicism over the past ten years. For these people, something had better "smell" completely different if they're going to allow themselves to care.

Ironically, as demands for greater involvement in our organizations increased, leaders of many well-publicized, large-scale change efforts moved the other way and totally ignored people. They chose instead to focus on more visible and seemingly easier-to-manage components such as information technology, strategic architectures, and business processes. Indeed, "Downsize" was a ubiquitous battle cry of the nineties. According to a 1996 *New York Times* poll, "Nearly three-quarters of all households have had a close encounter with layoffs since 1980. In one-third of all households, a family member has lost a job, and nearly 40 percent more know a relative, friend, or neighbor who was laid off."[2] The individual impact has been apparent in the increased stress, longer working hours, and reduced sense of job security chronicled in virtually every recent book and article on change.

To paraphrase Winston Churchill, "Never before in the field of human endeavors was so much screwed up by so few for so many." By ignoring the need to involve people in something that affects them, many of today's popular change methods have left a bad taste in the mouths of "change targets" (as one popular methodology calls those affected) for *any* type of change. They have also often left behind less effective organizations with fewer people and lower morale. Consequently, even well-intentioned, well-designed change efforts have a hard time getting off the ground.

If an organization or community's leaders *do* recognize that emerging values and rapidly shifting environmental demands call for directly engaging people in change, they often face another challenge. When the fear of uncertainty, the potential for winners and losers, and the history of failures define change, how can they systematically involve people and have some confidence that it will work? That is where this booklet comes in.

A Way Through

This booklet offers an approach that works because it acknowledges the prevailing attitudes toward change. It offers a fresh view based on the possibility of a more desirable future, experience with the whole system, and activities that signal "something different is happening this time." That difference systematically taps the potential of human beings to make themselves, their organizations, and their communities more adaptive and more effective. This approach is based on solid, proven principles for unleashing people's creativity, knowledge, and spirit toward a common purpose.

How can this be? It does so by filling two huge voids that most large-scale change efforts miss. The first improvement is *intelligently involving people* in changing their workplaces and communities. We have learned that creating a collective sense of purpose, sharing information traditionally known only to a few, valuing what people have to contribute, and inviting them to participate in meaningful ways positively affects outcomes. In other words, informed, engaged people can produce dramatic results.

The second improvement is a *systemic* approach to change. By asking "Who's affected? Who has a stake in this?" we begin to recognize that no change happens in isolation. Making the interdependencies explicit enables shifts based on a common view of the whole. We can each play our part while understanding our contribution to the system. We begin to understand that in a change effort the "one-party-wins-and-one-party-loses" perception need not necessarily be the case. When viewed from a systemic perspective, the lines between "winners" and "losers" become meaningless as everyone participates in cocreating the future for the betterment of all. The advantages are enormous: coordinated actions and closer relationships lead to simpler, more effective solutions.

The growing numbers of success stories are beginning to attract attention. Hundreds of examples around the world of dramatic and sustained increases in organization and community performance now exist.[3] With such great potential, why isn't everyone operating this way? The catch with high-involvement, systemic change is that more people have their say. Until traditional managers are ready to say yes to that, no matter how stunning the achievements of others, these approaches will remain out of reach for most and a competitive advantage for a few.

Our Purpose

This booklet describes an approach that has helped others achieve dramatic, sustainable results in their organization or communities. Our purpose is to provide basic information that you can use to decide whether this approach is right for you. We give you an overview including an illustrative story, answers to frequently asked questions and tips for getting started. We've also given you discussion questions for "thinking aloud" with others and a variety of references to learn more.

There is ample evidence that when high involvement and a system-wide approach are used, the potential for unimagined results is within reach. As Goethe so eloquently reminds us, "Whatever you can do or dream you can, begin it. Boldness has genius, power, and magic in it."

What are you waiting for?

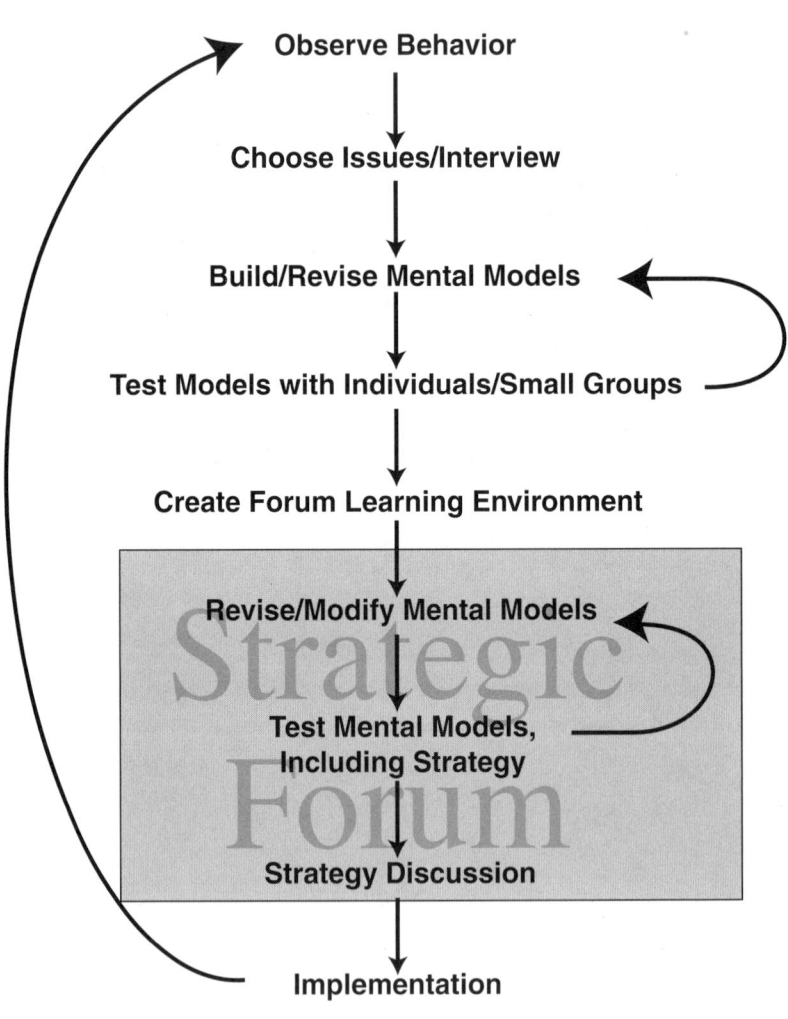

The Strategic Forum

Tell me, I forget.
Show me, I remember.
Involve me, I understand.

—ANCIENT CHINESE PROVERB

The Strategic Forum™ is a method for leading organizational and community change that utilizes the paradigms, tools, and methods of systems thinking. Systems thinking facilitates members of a system (where the system is an organization or community) in surfacing, challenging, and changing their understanding (also known as "mental models") of the key relationships that drive a system's ability to succeed-even survive. The remainder of this document provides the following useful information on Strategic Forums: examples of organizations and communities that have successfully applied Strategic Forums, an overview of necessary implementation steps, how to gauge an organization's or community's readiness for a Forum, and next steps to take if you wish to hold a Forum in your organization or community.

Two Stories

A Corporate Strategic Forum

During the mid-1980s, High Performance Systems, Inc. (HPS), performed a Strategic Forum for a small consulting firm (approximately

50 consultants). Barry Richmond, managing director of HPS, was hired by this spin-off boutique (a group of consultants from a large consulting firm who had spun off their own practice by taking some clients with them). High Performance Systems is a leader in systems thinking applications and was hired because of its ability to help organizations develop a clearer understanding of themselves through a systems thinking process called a Strategic Forum. The resulting Strategic Forum provided unique insight into both the company's operating goals and its strategy for achieving these goals.

The firm had established the following goals as critical success factors:

- Maintain healthy but aggressive company growth.
- Hire and develop the best and brightest young talent.
- Keep yearly attrition low (below 10 percent), i.e., don't let the talent leave.
- Maintain enough consultants to do the expected volume of work.

Its strategy for achieving these goals was as follows:

- Grow the business as an expanding pyramid, as in Figure 1 (i.e., maintain a 5:1 ratio of consultants to midlevel managers and keep the same ratio for midlevel managers to senior officers).
- Recruit from the most prestigious schools.
- Promise quick advancement (consultants were promised they would be midlevel managers within two to three years).

Recently, the firm had experienced difficulty keeping the head-count ratios at 5:1 and instituted a policy of increasing time between promotions. It questioned whether this strategy would pay off and wanted HPS to use a Strategic Forum to help answer this question.

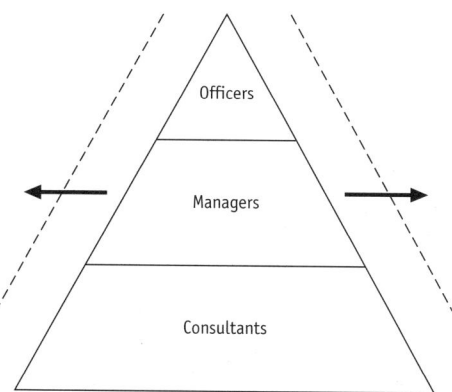

Figure 1. Grow the Business as an Expanding Pyramid

A few weeks before the Forum, facilitators from HPS interviewed various members of the management team. Using information from the interviews, we created a simple systems thinking model describing the "essence" of the human resource structure at the firm (shown in Figure 2).

The Strategic Forum utilizes a special language to facilitate discussion. The language is composed of stocks and flows. Stocks are like bathtubs that accumulate water (or people for this example), while flows are pipes that flow stuff into and out of stocks. In Figure 2, the

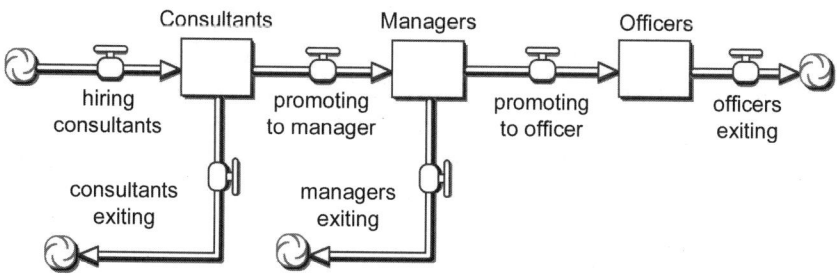

Figure 2. Systems Thinking Model Describing
the Human Resource Structure

rectangle labeled *Consultants* is a stock, which accumulates people, in this case the most junior members of the firm. *Consultants* flow into the organization through the activity of *hiring consultants* and enter the consultants stock. They remain consultants for some time and either flow on to managers by being promoted or flow out by exiting. The rest of the chain works similarly. Managers may flow up to officers or exit, and officers eventually leave.

At the Strategic Forum, 20 key managers and officers used computers to "fly" a model similar to Figure 2 using numbers that approximated the firm's real life experience. Even the simple model was able to replicate the behavior of pyramid flipping (too many officers and managers for the number of consultants) that they had been experiencing. The model was then modified to incorporate their understanding of what causes people to leave the organization. They were then able to try several strategies for achieving the four critical success factors mentioned previously. Working in small teams of four, they tried strategies they had used in real life and experimented with new ones.

The firm's operating goals (critical success factors) were inconsistent. *No* strategy could achieve all of them! The managers and officers discovered it would take an astronomical growth rate of 200 percent to maintain all other operating goals—which would cause the company to explode. Holding attrition at 10 percent (much lower than is common in large consulting firms) would necessitate employing the entire galaxy. And with a realistic growth rate, the pyramid would invert if the company maintained a swift-advancement policy.

The participants understood why their recent strategy of delaying promotions of consultants was creating unintended consequences. One consequence was an increase in the number of *consultants exiting* (refer to Figure 2) because they became frustrated at the lack of advancement. This led to a further unintended consequence: frustrated former employees told their colleagues from business school not to work for the firm. Because it had more difficulty hiring people, and more of the junior people were leaving, the firm found it had actually caused the recent inversion of the pyramid to accelerate. It had shot itself in the proverbial foot!

(In hindsight, it appears clear that these consequences would result from the firm's strategy and goals. However, such insight is not often available when it is needed, because our vision and thinking can become cloudy when we are in the middle of difficult situations. The Strategic Forum as described here helps give a perspective necessary to developing clearer thinking about an issue. The "Ah-ha's" of a Forum, although usually dramatic, are often met with "Of course, that's the way it is!")

Through the efforts of the Forum, the managers were finally able to see that their goals were inconsistent. Since they could not achieve all of them simultaneously, they discussed choosing from the following options:

1. Decide it was OK to have high attrition, as long as they could maintain the pyramid, in which case they could adopt policies common in many consulting firms (the "up or out" policy).
2. Encourage senior people to leave sooner.
3. Choose to let the pyramid flip. With more senior people than junior consultants, they could take on a lower volume of clients but perform more strategic work (with higher fees).

The knowledge gained at the Forum led to much better dialogue and, ultimately, better decision making. Shortly after the Forum, the firm was able to implement a combination of the modified goals listed above, and the corresponding strategies created the kind of successful, yet stable, consultancy it wanted.

A Community Strategic Forum

In 1993, HPS conducted a community-based Strategic Forum for a school system undergoing heated debate about a proposed school policy that would impact the entire community. The policy was to implement year-round schooling. Members of the community (decision makers, business leaders, teachers, parents) were gathered for the Forum and given an opportunity to experiment with various computer models representing how this policy would affect the students, teachers, and ultimately the community.

The process began by looking at a model of retained content (Figure 3). Stakeholders agreed that the process of content retention could be modeled as a stock of retained content with an inflow of assimilating content and an outflow of losing content. The first part of the Forum was designed to answer this question: Would students who attend school year-round retain content better? To answer it, the Forum participants needed to reach consensus on what allowed students to assimilate content (the inflow), and what forces caused them to lose (forget) content (the outflow). The map shown in Figure 3 kept the discussion rich yet focused.

By simulating an expanded model based on the above map, the participants decided the policy would likely improve content retention. The Forum facilitator further expanded the model to include various impacts of the year-round policy on student culture (e.g., the impact on school discipline), teacher effectiveness, and the community economy. As community impacts were added, the participants saw that although the policy would appear beneficial to the students, it would have unintended consequences on the community economy. Specifically, a town that relied on employing students during the summer would

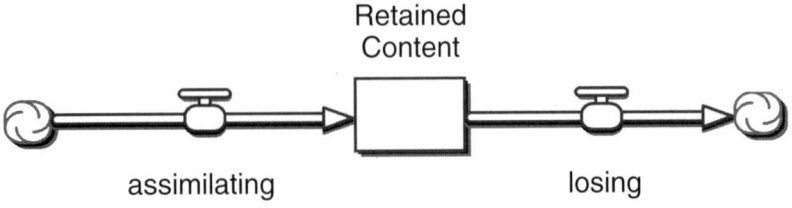

Figure 3. Systems Thinking Model of Retained Content

need to compensate for the potential loss of labor since student labor would be in school. Understanding the negative consequences on the community helped the Forum participants decide against the policy. By slowly adding different impacts, allowing stakeholders to experiment and question the models and providing an opportunity for community dialogue, the Forum facilitated the community's movement through a polarized political debate to reaching community consensus.

Why a Strategic Forum?

The structure of any social organization (business, nonprofit, or community), its mission, goals, and strategies—why and how it organizes itself—result from that organization's individual and collective *mental models*. Mental models are the collection of assumptions, theories, anecdotes, and other mental facts and images used to make sense of complex systems (and most of life is complex!) and make decisions. Many of these mental models remain unspoken and untested—yet they drive the organization's behavior. The Strategic Forum is a process that allows an organization to uncover, clarify, and modify the mental models driving its most fundamental processes.

Using a systems thinking approach, key stakeholders in a system use a Strategic Forum to develop a clear picture of how that system fits together—its mission, goals, and strategies—into an integrated whole. The systems thinking approach includes a language (the stock/flow language mentioned before) that facilitates surfacing and clarifying mental models. Systems thinking can improve mental models because the language enforces a discipline of looking at and understanding the interrelationships that are often overlooked in analyzing an organization or community. Relationships drive behavior, so understanding the relationships in the organization or community is the key to finding high-leverage solutions.

A Forum helps uncover the essence of how the system really "works," how a strategy will unfold within the context of that system, or both. The skill of understanding how something does (or will) work is *operational thinking*. Developing an operational picture helps bring to light any misalignment or fuzzy thinking embedded in an organization's goals, strategies, and processes. Organizational goals are often not independent, as the consulting firm in the case example found. In some situations, two goals might be impossible to achieve— achieving one goal might preclude achieving another goal. In other situations, a strategy might be impossible to implement. For example, one sales department discovered through a Forum that a strategy to double revenue by doubling the sales force, although sounding good in the abstract, was impractical. A strategy that seems certain to succeed at an off-site retreat might never be capable of achieving its intended purpose back in the organization. A Strategic Forum will reveal any inconsistent goal or point out if a strategy cannot achieve what it's designed to do.

The Strategic Forum Process: An Overview

The process begins by having each stakeholder (senior manager, policymaker, civic leader) bring out and clarify his or her view of the mission, goals, and strategies for that organization or community. This is referred to as "surfacing one's individual mental model about the business/community." (Each stakeholder has a mental model of the system, which is often unconscious and rarely discussed at any depth.) The process continues using stocks and flows to build a coherent visual map or collective mental model. This means that stakeholders develop a consensus about how the organization works. The map is constantly refined, through several iterations of presentation and feedback, until it is the most useful representation of the organization for analyzing the operating goals and strategies. This map is then turned into a "simulatable" model or models.

The Strategic Forum provides a forum (pun intended) to allow stakeholders to systematically interact with the model, testing their various assumptions about the goals and strategies. As they do, they begin to see any holes (from tiny to gaping) in their understanding of how the organization "works" or how a strategy might actually unfurl. These holes are used to generate discussion, and this discussion often results in the stakeholders' revising their collective mental models about goals and/or strategies.

The resulting product of a Forum is usually a model or series of models that can be packaged for consumption by the rest of the system. For example, a community forum could result in a CD-ROM "game" that allows citizens to manage their community. Citizens who manage their community in a game would generate a better understanding of how their community works, which would help policymakers and citizens develop and support policies that will improve their community. Sometimes these models are given out on CD-ROMs; other times they are presented at a facilitated session. For example, as the result of a Strategic Forum, a large global computer manufacturer developed a facilitated workshop that it delivered to its top sales managers around the world. By sharing models that have been developed through a Forum and/or by developing systems thinking capacity within the organization, the effects of a Strategic Forum will ripple out to the rest of the organization.

Organizational Changes Resulting from a Strategic Forum

Because a Forum helps an organization develop an operational understanding of its mission, goals, and systems, a post-Forum organization will always have a clearer picture of how it really works—what can and cannot be done to improve its performance. Also, as a result of unearthing and sharing mental models, individuals throughout the system learn to communicate more effectively. Individuals and teams (even the collective public) realize that all mental models, because they are always simplistic representations of reality, are wrong. The people become more willing to enter into open dialogue for the purpose of learning from each other. By being able to more fully utilize systems thinking to make all assumptions explicit and then test them with computer simulation, the organization moves toward becoming a learning organization.

When Should an Organization Use a Strategic Forum?

A Strategic Forum can be used at any point in the strategy development process for various reasons:

- prior to developing a strategy, as a vehicle to clarify its mission and goals, as well as determine some of the key issues a strategy must address;
- during strategy development as *the* strategy process;
- after developing a strategy, where it serves as a "sanity check" on the recently developed strategy.

Likely Outcomes of a Strategic Forum

Businesses and communities usually revise—sometimes abandon—their goals and strategies. They realize that many of their assumptions (usually held as self-evident truths) that led to previous goals and strategies were incomplete or erroneous. They may realize they weren't even asking the right questions. After a Strategic Forum, an organization is better able to ask the right questions, thus improving any subsequent goal-forming and strategy-making process.

Since this process surfaces and challenges myriad cultural assumptions, the impact can be dramatic. Organizations emerge from the Forum less likely to blame problems on external factors. They shift from focusing on events to looking for patterns over time. Organizations stop blaming people and instead seek to understand the underlying structure that might be causing disturbing behavior. Community members stop blaming politicians for problems once they see how they, too, contribute to those problems. They are less likely to focus only on short-term consequences and begin to consider potential long-term consequences. Finally, individuals and groups move from focusing on my (our) "piece of the pie" to looking at the whole pie.

The Steps in the Process

The following diagram is a high-level representation of the steps an organization takes when participating in a Strategic Forum. The actual steps taken are rarely as neat as described here. Usually there is some jumping around in the process, often cycling through several of the steps more than once. The essence of a Forum—what really happens—is described in Figure 4.

The organization members start either by *Observing Behavior* or by *Choosing Issues* to explore, if they have a strategy they want to "sanity-check" (which really means to examine a strategy's ability to achieve

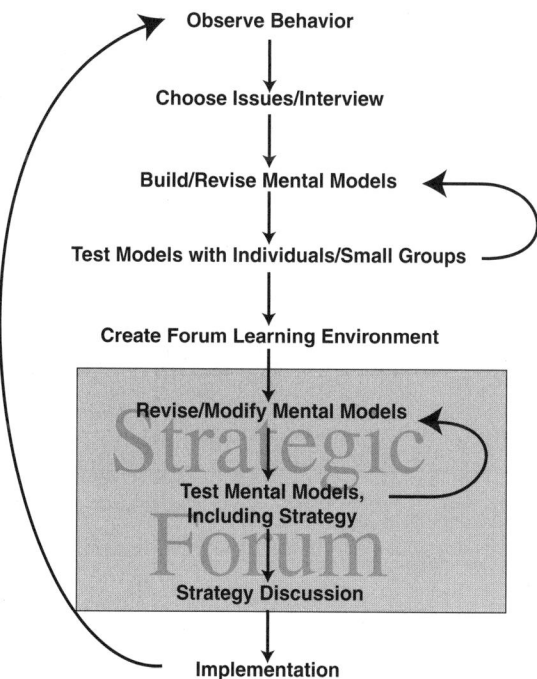

Figure 4. High-Level Representation of Strategic Forum

its intended result). In the *Observe Behavior* step, an example of observing behavior includes the organization mentioned in the first example, which identified the need for a Forum because they noticed consultant attrition had been climbing in recent months. An example of checking a strategy's effectiveness might occur with a community looking at the policies it is implementing to slow urban growth. Both steps are done in the pre-Forum phases, which begin somewhere between eight to sixteen weeks prior to the Forum.

Once the organization or community identifies its need for a Forum, they usually locate an expert to help them through the process. The choice is critical. The facilitator must possess both process skills (understand how a Forum works), as well as systems thinking skills (the ability to build and communicate informative simulation models). The facilitator will initially revisit the issue or strategy the organization or community wishes to address (as a group and in individual *Interviews*), making sure a Forum is the appropriate tool.

The *Build/Revise Mental Models* phase begins with a brief training in systems thinking skills. This initiates the process of developing capacity within the organization or community, with the ultimate goal being that they (the organization or community) will eventually be able to hold Forums or apply systems thinking in the future without outside expertise. The training can be with as many members of the organization or community as desired—in one organization over sixty people received appropriate training. However, after the training a small team of modelers (usually three to six) forms to begin model building. This is when they begin building and revising their and other members' mental models through the language of stocks and flows.

The team then *Tests the Model(s) with Individuals/Small Groups* in order to clarify and modify the assumptions embedded in their model(s). The team learns a great deal through this step, both with respect to what is needed to improve the model (perhaps they were missing a key relationship), as well as how to engage others in the organization with the model. All of this information will be valuable in *Creating the Forum Learning Environment* (LE). The LE is a computer-based teaching tool designed to facilitate interaction with the model(s) and the subsequent discussion of insights generated by the model(s). The development of the model(s) and LE usually takes the team and facilitator(s) one to three months, depending on the amount of time the team can devote to the development.

Once the LE has been created, the system members (of the organization or community) are ready to hold the Strategic Forum, a one- or two-day session where important stakeholders are gathered to interact with the LE and discuss the implication on the system. The Forum usually begins by revisiting the purpose of the Forum and reviewing the agenda for the session (these should already be known prior to the session). Next, teams of three to five are instructed on how to interact with the LE. This is the *Revise/Modify Mental Models* and *Test Mental Models, Including Strategy* steps. For example, teams in a community forum might be instructed to try various strategies to improve the local education system. They would then test one strategy at a time, view a simulation of the strategy's impact, and then discuss the implication. Eventually, the small groups would reconvene in a large group, where a facilitator leads a discussion of group findings and implications. This process of small-group interactions leading to large-group discussion will iterate several times. It is designed to build a collective and clarified mental model of the system.

Once the group's mental model has been sufficiently clarified, it is time for *Strategy Discussion.* Because the session helped the group build a collective mental model, they will find their ability to discuss and develop strategy is greatly improved. In a pharmaceutical organization, after interacting with a model describing how new drugs are marketed, the sales team was better able to put their resources on a high-leverage activity (which turned out to be keeping clients happy, not getting unhappy clients back). In the case of a community, because community members will share an improved mental model of how the economy, education, and other public services are connected, they will be more likely to understand the implications of various policies and support the one(s) with the best consequences for the overall community.

Implementation occurs after the Forum. Usually three things occur during the implementation phase. First, the organization or community begins implementing the strategy developed during the Forum. Sometimes the implementation takes the form of a pilot study. Second, the insights generated at the Forum need to be shared with the rest of the organization or community. Often this is done through the LE (or a modified version of it) that is used at organization or community sessions similar to the original Forum. One multinational organization shared a Forum LE with hundreds of its top sales managers worldwide. Third, the process of developing systems thinking capacity is continued. Members of the organization or community will continue skill building in systems thinking by developing models, applying them to issues, and perhaps cycling through more Strategic Forums. If implemented correctly, the process should be adopted as part of an ongoing process of learning and improvement.

To assess the value of a Strategic Forum, consider the cost to an organization of pursuing goals it cannot achieve or of using strategies that cannot achieve intended goals. Once the Strategic Forum is put into the above perspective, it is easy to justify its costs. An organization can waste years of time, countless labor hours, and precious resources on the impossible, or it can put a little of each into a Strategic Forum and become more confident that what it is working on is possible.

Successfully Implementing a Strategic Forum

There are many key ingredients to making a Strategic Forum successful. Here are some of the more important ones:

- *Be open to analyzing your thinking.* The core process underlying the Strategic Forum is to surface inaccuracies and inconsistencies in individual and collective mental models. Senior leaders need to be willing to expose and analyze their own mental models or the process is likely to fail.

- *Look at the big picture.* People often see only their small piece of the world; the process of building a collective understanding of the organization naturally causes individuals and groups within the organization to see the whole more clearly. Groups that have been unable to understand how another group could see the problem "that way" suddenly get the experience of stepping into the others' shoes. This has tremendous beneficial effects on overall trust and communication within the whole system.

- *Don't expect to discover the "truth."* Mental models are always a simplification of reality and by definition are not the truth. Much confusion can result when participants expect the process to uncover truth. The Forum helps participants discover "holes" in their individual and collective mental models. Just as the scientific method says that all theories can at best be entertainable, at worst disconfirmed, so a Forum will show which mental model is most congruent with reality. It (the mental model) will never be reality, however.

- *Keep the map/model small.* The type of model—large, complex, unwieldy—resulting from truth-seeking is usually impossible to build (at the level of detail where each participant can describe his or her part of the system) and is always impossible to discuss. Arie de Geus, in a preface to *Modeling for Learning Organizations* (a book of collected articles describing how to apply computer modeling techniques to businesses), says, "Even the simplest business has so many internal and external interrelationships, to which new ones are added all the time, that it is most unlikely that the model describing a company will ever be finished."[1] Going down this path will cause the Forum process to stall.

Roles, Responsibilities, Relationships

The roles, responsibilities, and relationships in the Strategic Forum are summarized in the table below.

Impact on Power and Authority

Often decisions are made based strictly upon financial considerations, giving those portions of the organization monitoring its financial aspects a higher degree of influence. The Strategic Forum method will cause the organization to look at its business in terms of soft variables

	Pre-Forum	*Forum*	*Post-Forum*
Sponsor(s) (senior leaders or process owners)	• Learn about Forum and be committed • Define process and issues for Forum • Gather stake-holders • Take part in model development	• Attend Forum • Provide context when necessary • Participate in model experi-mentation with participants	• Change mission, goals, and strate-gies as dictated by Forum • Develop next steps for incorporating Forum results into rest of organization
Facilitator/ Designer (may be two people: one focusing on the group process, the other focusing on modeling)	• Meet with sponsor and participants • Learn issues • Build preliminary model(s) and re-vise with feedback • Design Forum	• Facilitate Forum • Focus on uncover-ing assumptions of all attendees • Revise session and/or model as necessary	• Work with spon-sor as appropriate to design next steps (e.g., build a learning environ-ment of models or design follow-up sessions)
Participants (process stakeholders)	• Meet with sponsor and facilitator • Meet alone and in groups • Provide input into model	• Work in teams to explore model(s) • Participate in group discussion	• Implement changes dictated by Forum

Table 1. Roles, Responsibilities, and Relationships

(such as morale, skill level, and innovation capability), as well as hard ones (such as financials and inventory). This results in a leveling effect, where power is shared more across the organization. Groups such as human resources or research and development become more important to understanding how the business really works.

One financial services company HPS worked with had a strategy of periodic sales "blitzes" for loans that were implemented by the marketing department. The intended consequence was to increase the amount of money on loan and thus increase revenues. The unintended consequence was that due to the increased number of loans and the resulting lower average loan amount, the administrative department was incurring huge expenses, which actually made the loans unprofitable. As a result of a Forum where members from each department experienced this phenomenon, the once all-powerful marketing department realized it needed to communicate with, not dictate to, other departments within the organization: a leveling in power occurred.

Sometimes in the process of designing a Forum, senior managers realize that important information is held by people lower in the organization. The nature of the process requires these knowledge holders to be included in the modeling and Forum process. This creates an environment where senior managers learn to distribute power not only across but also down into the organization.

Do's and Don'ts

Do use a Strategic Forum when

- groups are rushing down the solution path and haven't made sure they've chosen the right problem to address.
- discussion of a strategy has not resulted in a consensus.
- there is a need to look at nonphysical variables (e.g., morale, motivation, employee skill, community health, and customer satisfaction) and their impact on the system. One strength of

systems thinking is that the language and technology can work just as easily with variables such as motivation and customer satisfaction as they can with finances and head count.

- it's important to see the impact of a strategy over wide space and time bounds. Strategies implemented today might have unintended consequences several years down the road or in distant parts of the organization or community.

Don't use a Strategic Forum when

- you can't find a competent system dynamics modeler. The models that are used in the Forum must resemble the participants' understanding, be simple, and provide some counterintuitive insights. The skills required to do this are not common and are crucial to making the process a success.
- there is little time for discussion (i.e., an emergency requires quick decisions) or if you can't get the whole system involved in the discussion.
- it is considered an event—a one-time occurrence that will significantly solve the organization's problems. The power of the Forum is not in the answers it can unfurl but in the coincident dialogue it can generate.
- the organization is unwilling to embrace an ongoing systems thinking approach and skill set. An organization often finds itself in trouble because of the collective mental models it has been using to make decisions. These models often result from a nonsystemic paradigm set. Adopting a systems thinking paradigm is the best safeguard an organization can develop against creating similar conditions in the future.

More About System Dynamics and Systems Thinking

Systems thinking is the art and science of understanding how structure determines performance so that one may use that understanding to change structure to improve performance. The structure includes an organization's processes and systems, explicit and implicit policies (including mission, strategies, and goals), and culture, all of which result from mental models.

The Strategic Forum is a logical extension of system dynamics. The field of system dynamics was developed largely from the efforts of Jay Forrester at the Massachusetts Institute of Technology (MIT). During the 1960s and 1970s, Professor Forrester and his colleagues created a large body of work in social dynamics that has been applied to industrial, urban, and world systems.

Barry Richmond, the managing director of HPS, is one of Forrester's colleagues. Richmond received his doctorate in system dynamics from MIT and has pioneered the development of the Strategic Forum as a framework for organizational change. Over the years, Richmond and his colleagues at HPS have delivered nearly 50 Strategic Forums in a variety of businesses and communities. Using experience gained in these Forums, he has continued to refine the approach described in this booklet.

Systems thinking (popularized by Peter Senge) is a term that many use interchangeably with system dynamics. Many people have used systems thinking as the foundation for organizational change. For the sake of simplicity, there are two distinct approaches taken by systems thinking practitioners: *modeling* and *conversational mapping*. The modeling approach is to work with the client organization to develop a model of the organization—usually to a high level of detail. The modeler interviews the client, develops a detailed model, analyzes it for insights, and prepares a final report outlining the findings and suggestions for organizational change. This approach results in a simulatable model that can be rigorously tested for validity, but usually creates a "black box" model—a model where all of the assumptions made by the modeler remain hidden from anyone who uses it—which inhibits learning about the very system the model is trying to explain. In summary, the modeler usually creates a good, rigorous, insightful product (the model), but the process is lacking—in this case it leaves the client unengaged.

Mappers focus more on group process when they approach a problem. They gather the decision makers in a room and facilitate the development of a causal loop diagram, focusing on key feedback relationships in the system(s) of interest. However, causal loop diagrams (a favorite of most mappers) do not provide a rigorous method for testing—they cannot simulate. Therefore, little can be done to sanity-check findings that result from a mapper's approach. The process is great for collaborating, but the product (the map) is less helpful for generating insights.

The Strategic Forum combines these two approaches in a way that blends their strengths and eliminates or reduces their weaknesses. It provides both a *process* for keeping clients involved—they remain right at the point of learning each step of the way—and a highly useful *product* for rigorously testing the joint mental model developed. The models at the Forum are relatively small and easy to understand, and clients are involved in developing them along the way. Because they employ the stock/flow language, they are simulatable. Participants are able to see their mental models in action and can change their assumptions during the process.

Post-Forum Activities

We recommend the following post-Forum activities:

- Disseminate Forum insights.
- Develop in-house systems thinking capability.

Sometimes a Forum will suggest other stakeholders who need to be involved in the process. This helps to both disseminate key learning and engage the organization in implementing new strategies. In one organization, a Strategic Forum resulted in a subsequent Forum's being delivered to a subset of the organization, which required further refinement to the maps used in the first Forum. With respect to developing systems thinking capability, an organization will find that one Forum is not enough to embed this approach and language in the culture.

A good goal, as mentioned in the section on likely outcomes, is to develop an ongoing organizational learning process, in which the best thinking in the organization is captured and refined in a library of models. One client developed an internal resource team responsible for developing and maintaining a library of models concerning a strategy for improving the product development cycle. This team successfully worked with several other teams to create models that covered the gamut from how to develop tools more rapidly to what the organization would "feel" like as it experienced different aspects of the change effort. Currently it is using these models to engage the rest of the organization to further refine and develop how it accomplishes its process-improvement goals.

Notes

· ·

Introduction

[1] Oakley, Ed, and Doug Krug. *Enlightened Leadership.* Denver, Colo.: Stone Tree Publishing, 1991, p. 38.

[2] The *New York Times, The Downsizing of America.* New York: Times Books, 1996.

[3] Holman, Peggy, and Tom Devane, eds. *The Change Handbook: Group Methods for Shaping the Future.* San Francisco: Berrett-Koehler Publishers, 1999. This book contains over twenty such stories of stellar results from high-involvement, systemic change.

The Strategic Forum

[1] de Geus, Arie. Foreword to *Modeling for Learning Organizations,* edited by J.D.W. Morecroft and J. D. Sterman. Portland, Oreg.: Productivity Press, 1994, p. xiv.

Where to Go for More Information

. . . .

Since our focus has been to give you an introduction to the Strategic Forum, we want you to know where to go for more information. Here are books, articles, Web sites, and other sources that can help you develop a more in-depth understanding. In addition, we have provided recommendations of works that have influenced the author.

Organizations

High Performance Systems, Inc.
45 Lyme Road, Suite 200
Hanover, NJ 03755
(603) 643-9636
(603) 643-9502 (fax)
support@hps-inc.com (e-mail)
www.hps-inc.com (Web site)
• Workshops • Consulting services

Pontifex Consulting
One Smith Road
Hanover, NJ 03755
(603) 653-0228
(603) 653-0323 (fax)
chris.s.soderquist@pontifexconsulting.com (e-mail)
www.pontifexconsulting.com
• Consulting services • Facilitation • Training

Pegasus Communications, Inc.
One Moody Street
Waltham, MA 02453
(781) 398-9700
(781) 894-7175 (fax)
Mktg@Pegasuscom.com (e-mail)
www.pegasuscom.com (Web site)
• Clearinghouse for Systems Thinking materials

The Strategic Forum References

Richmond, B. "The Strategic Forum: Aligning Objectives, Strategy and
   Process." *System Dynamics Review* 13 (Summer 1997): 131–148.
   The seminal article on the Strategic Forum by the person responsible
   for developing it.
———, et al. *ithink© Business Applications Guide.* High Performance
   Systems, 1997.
   Software documentation filled with many real-life applications of
   Systems Thinking.

Influential Sources

Forrester, J. W. *Industrial Dynamics.* Portland, Oreg.: Productivity Press,
   1961.
   The seminal book in the system dynamics field. Published in 1961 and
   just as relevant today.
Morecroft, J.D.W., and J. D. Sterman. *Modeling for Learning
   Organizations.* Portland, Ore.: Productivity Press, 1994.
   A great reference for how modeling has been used in a variety of
   contexts. Very practical.
Senge, Peter M. *The Fifth Discipline: The Art & Practice of the Learning
   Organization.* New York: Currency Doubleday, 1990.

Questions for Thinking Aloud

· ·

To gain additional value from this booklet, consider discussing it with others. Here are some questions you might find useful as you explore Strategic Forum and its application to your situation.

1. What were your reasons for reading about the Strategic Forum? What situation(s) did you have in mind as possible applications? What, if any, trends have you noticed in your organization (for example, your best talent leaving) or community (for example, urban sprawl) that are troubling? How might a Strategic Forum help you better resolve them?

2. A Strategic Forum helps uncover the essence of how the system really "works," and/or how a strategy will unfold within that system. What are the current strategies your organization/community employs? How do these strategies interact? How well do they complement each other?

3. A Strategic Forum can be used to clarify an organization or community's mission and goals, develop strategy, or affirm a strategy's viability. How would you decide if a Strategic Forum could help your organization or community?

4. How would a Strategic Forum work in your culture? What strengths might it take advantage of? What barriers exist that might impede the effectiveness of a Forum?

5. Who are the key stakeholders in the system you wish to improve? Will they be willing to work on a Forum with you? What might preclude their willingness?

6. If you think a Forum is an appropriate method for your organization or community, what are your next steps?

The Author

. . . .

Chris Soderquist is the founder of Pontifex Consulting, a firm whose mission is to use Systems Thinking and developmental facilitation to build the capacity of individuals and organizations to understand and improve systems by developing high-leverage solutions. He has practical experience working with various organizations, including Fortune 500 companies, small businesses, government organizations, and nonprofits. Prior to founding his own company, Chris was a consultant at High Performance Systems, Inc. (HPS), a company specializing in Systems Thinking tools and techniques. While at HPS, Chris, along with Barry Richmond, coauthored *Systems Thinking: Taking the Next Step,* an interactive computer learning environment designed to teach the practical application of Systems Thinking to a wide audience. He has also worked for the U.S. Treasury Department as both a statistician and an organizational development facilitator. Chris is currently working to further develop and refine the tools and techniques of the Strategic Forum for use in the public sector, believing that Forums hold tremendous promise for improving policy making and public participation.

Series Editors
Peggy Holman is a writer and consultant who helps organizations achieve cultural transformation. High involvement and a whole-systems perspective characterize her work. Her clients include AT&T Wireless

Services, Weyerhaeuser Company, St. Joseph's Medical Center, and the U.S. Department of Labor. Peggy can be reached at (425) 746-6274 or pholman@msn.com.

Tom Devane is an internationally known consultant and speaker specializing in transformation. He helps companies plan and implement transformations that utilize highly participative methods to achieve sustainable change. His clients include Microsoft, Hewlett-Packard, AT&T, Johnson & Johnson, and the Republic of South Africa. Tom can be reached at (303) 898-6172 or tdevane@iex.net.

The Change Handbook

Group Methods for Shaping the Future

Edited by Peggy Holman and Tom Devane

The Change Handbook presents eighteen proven, highly successful change methods that enable organizations and communities of all shapes and sizes to engage and focus the energy and commitment of all their members These diverse participative change approaches, described in detail by their creators and expert practitioners, illustrate how organizations and communities today can achieve and sustain extraordinary results and foster a capacity to handle the inevitable turbulence along the way. By first systematically involving all organizational stakeholders in the change process, and then planning and implementing change simultaneously—in real time—these methods uniquely enable all members to become change agents, active participants in determining their organization's direction and future.

Marvin Weisbord, Merrelyn Emery, Masaaki Imai, Kathie Dannemiller, Harrison Owen, and many other leading thinkers and practitioners of organizational change show how to harness the vision, energy, and enthusiasm of the entire organization—from employees at all levels to key stakeholders to entire communities. In *The Change Handbook* they provide practical answers to frequently asked questions to that you can choose the methods that will work best in your participative change efforts.

> *"In a world where change is the norm, where the effectiveness of organizations is a competitive advantage, and where we have more change methodologies available than most people could absorb in a lifetime, this book has identified how to match the best approach to the situation. While providing structured guidelines for organizational improvement, the authors acknowledge and celebrate the power of creativity and engaged people to provide the energy needed for successful change."*
>
> —SUSAN MERSEREAU, *Vice President,*
> *Organizational Effectiveness, Weyerhaeuser Company*

Paperback original, approx. 450 pages, ISBN 1-57675-058-2

Item no. 50582-605   U.S. $49.95

To order call 800-929-2929 or visit www.bkconnection.com

Collaborating for Change

Peggy Holman and Tom Devane, Editors

The Collaborating for Change booklet series offers concise, comprehensive overviews of 14 leading change strategies in a convenient, inexpensive format. Adapted from chapters in *The Change Handbook*, each booklet is written by the originator of the change strategy or an expert practitioner, and includes

- An example of the strategy in action
- Tips for getting started
- An outline of roles, responsibilities, and relationships
- Conditions for success
- Keys to sustaining results
- Thought-provoking questions for discussion

If you're deciding on a change strategy for your organization and you need a short, focused treatment of several alternatives to distribute to your colleagues, or you've decided on a change strategy and want to disseminate information about it to get everyone on board, the Collaborating for Change booklets are the ideal choice.

◆ SEARCH CONFERENCE
Merrelyn Emery and Tom Devane
Uses open systems principles in strategic planning, thereby creating a well-articulated, achievable future with identifiable goals, a timetable, and action plans for realizing that future.

◆ FUTURE SEARCH
Marvin R. Weisbord and Sandra Janoff
Helps members of an organization or community discover common ground and create self-managed plans to move toward their desired future.

◆ THE CONFERENCE MODEL
Emily M. Axelrod and Richard H. Axelrod
Engages the critical mass needed for success in redesigning organizations and processes, co-creating a vision of the future, improving customer and supplier relationships, or achieving strategic alignment.

◆ THE WHOLE SYSTEMS APPROACH
Cindy Adams and W. A. (Bill) Adams
Creates a world of work where people and organizations thrive and produce outrageous individual and organizational results.

◆ PREFERRED FUTURING
Lawrence L. Lippitt
Mobilizes everyone involved in a human system to envision the future they want and then develop strategies to get there.

◆ THE STRATEGIC FORUM
Chris Soderquist
Answers "Can our strategy achieve our objectives?" by building shared understanding (a mental map) of how the organization or community really works.

◆ PARTICIPATIVE DESIGN WORKSHOP
Merrelyn Emery and Tom Devane
Enables an organization to function in an interrelated structure of self-managing work groups.

◆ GEMBA KAIZEN
Masaaki Imai and Brian Heymans
Builds a culture able to initiate and sustain change by providing skills to improve process, enabling employees to make daily improvements, installing JIT systems and lean process methods in administrative systems, and improving equipment reliability and product quality.

◆ THE ORGANIZATION WORKSHOP
Barry Oshry and Tom Devane
Develops the knowledge and skills of "system sight" that enable us to create partnerships up, down, and across organizational lines.

◆ WHOLE-SCALE CHANGE
Kathleen D. Dannemiller, Sylvia L. James, and Paul D. Tolchinsky
Helps organizations remain successful through fast, deep, and sustainable total system change by bringing members together as one-brain (all seeing the same things) and one-heart (all committed to achieving the same preferred future).

◆ OPEN SPACE TECHNOLOGY
Harrison Owen (with Anne Stadler)
Enables high levels of group interaction and productivity to provide a basis for enhanced organizational function over time.

◆ APPRECIATIVE INQUIRY
David L. Cooperrider and Diana Whitney
Supports full-voiced appreciative participation in order to tap an organization's positive change core and inspire collaborative action that serves the whole system.

◆ THINK LIKE A GENIUS PROCESS
Todd Siler
Helps individuals and organizations go beyond narrow, compartmentalized thinking; improve communication, teamwork, and collaboration; and achieve breakthrough thinking.

◆ REAL TIME STRATEGIC CHANGE
Robert W. Jacobs and Frank McKeown
Uses large, interactive group meetings to rapidly create an organization's preferred future and then sustain it over time.

Collaborating for Change Order Form
Each booklet comes shrinkwrapped in packets of 6

Order in Quantity and Save!
1–4 packets: $45 per packet • 5–9 packets: $40.50 per packet
10–49 packets: $38.25 per packet • 50–99 packets: $36 per packet

# of Packets		Item #	Price
_____	*Search Conference*	6058X-605	_____
_____	*Future Search*	60598-605	_____
_____	*The Strategic Forum*	60601-605	_____
_____	*Participative Design Workshop*	6061X-605	_____
_____	*Gemba Kaizen*	60628-605	_____
_____	*The Whole Systems Approach*	60636-605	_____
_____	*Preferred Futuring*	60644-605	_____
_____	*The Organization Workshop*	60652-605	_____
_____	*Whole-Scale Change*	60660-605	_____
_____	*Open Space Technology*	60679-605	_____
_____	*Appreciative Inquiry*	60687-605	_____
_____	*The Conference Model*	60695-605	_____
_____	*Think Like a Genius Process*	60709-605	_____
_____	*Real Time Strategic Change*	60717-605	_____

Shipping and Handling _____
($4.50 for the first packet; $1.50 for each additional packet.)

TOTAL (CA residents add sales tax) $_____

Method of Payment
Orders payable in U.S. dollars. Orders outside U.S. and Canada must be prepaid.

❏ Payment enclosed ❏ Visa ❏ MasterCard ❏ American Express

Card no. _____ Expiration date _____

Signature _____

Name _____ Title _____

Organization _____

Address _____

City/State/Zip _____

Phone (in case we have questions about your order) _____

May we notify you about new Berrett-Koehler products and special offers via e-mail?

E-mail _____

Send Orders to Berrett-Koehler Communications, Inc., P.O. Box 565,
Williston, VT 05495 • **Fax** (802) 864-7626 • **Phone** (800) 929-2929
• **Web** www.bkconnection.com